STICKER ENCYCLOPEDIA
Dinosaurs

LONDON, NEW YORK, MUNICH,
MELBOURNE, AND DELHI

Written by Dougal Dixon
Edited by Sarah Davis
US Editor Margaret Parrish
Designed by Chloe Luxford
Jacket Designer Chloe Luxford
Design Assistants Wendy Bartlet, Fiona Gowen,
Polly Appleton
Picture Research Chloe Luxford, Kate Lockley
Illustration by Peter Bull
Globes supplied by DK Cartography
Design Development Manager Helen Senior
Publishing Manager Becky Hunter
Associate Publisher Sue Leonard
Production Editor Andy Hilliard
Production Man Fai Lau

First published in the United States
in 2009 by DK Publishing
345 Hudson Street
New York, New York 10014

13 12 11 10
015-SD434 – Aug/2009

The publisher would like to thank the following for their kind permission to reproduce their photographs:

(Key: a-above; b-below/bottom; c-center; f-far; l-left; r-right; t-top)

Corbis: Louie Psihoyos 35br, 35cr, 44c, 54bl. **DK Images:** Bedrock Studios 4bc, 10c;
Robert L. Braun - modelmaker 1br, 4crb, 5fcl, 6fclb (background), 15c, 44fcl, 47bl, 48-49 (background);
Centaur Studios - modelmakers 21crb, 27c, 51cr; David Donkin - modelmaker 4bl, 4cl, 4clb; Graham High
at Centaur Studios - modelmaker 4cb, 4fcr, 15cra, 26-27; Jon Hughes / Bedrock Studios 1c, 3t (background),
5c, 5fbr, 5fcr, 5fcrb, 9r (background); Jonathan Hately - modelmaker 1cl; John Holmes - modelmaker 2br
(background); Jeremy Hunt at Centaur Studios - modelmaker 15ftr, 24cl; Natural History Museum, London
3bl, 3cra, 4fbl, 15fbl, 16-17 (background), 28c (background), 39crb, 41c, 44fbl, 45tr; Peabody Museum
of Natural History, Yale University. 45cla; Luis Rey - modelmaker 4cr, 36-37 (background); Royal Tyrrell
Museum of Palaeontology, Alberta, Canada 2tl (background), 20bl (background), 42-43 (background),
54-55; Sedgwick Museum of Geology, Cambridge 30-31 (background); Gary Staab - modelmaker 5bl, 7cl
(background); Staatliches Museum fur Naturkunde, Stuttgart 11c; State Museum of Nature, Stuttgart 54cla;
Dennis Wilson - modelmaker 44cr. **Getty Images:** Altrendo Nature 26bc; De Agostini Picture Library / DEA
Picture Library 46clb (background); CGIBackgrounds.com 26br; Digital Vision / Sylvester Adams 26clb;
Bruno Morandi 26cl; National Geographic / Jeffrey L. Osborn 22-23 (background), 40tl; Taxi / Michael
Duva 26cb; Visuals Unlimited / Ken Lucas 27r. **Sticker fun backgrounds: Getty Images:** Altrendo Nature
(lake scene); CGIBackgrounds.com (woodland plains scene); Digital Vision / Sylvester Adams (desert
scene); Bruno Morandi (sea scene); Taxi / Michael Duva (riverside forest scene). **Stickers: Alamy Images:**
Oleksiy Maksymenko 5fbr (skeleton). **Corbis:** Louie Psihoyos 3ftl (fossil), 7c (teeth), 10fclb (teeth), 12fcl
(fossil), 15cb (teeth), 16ftl (fossil), 16tr (teeth). **DK Images:** American Museum of Natural History 4tl
(skeleton), 5fcla (skeleton); Bedrock Studios 7cl (T-rex); Centaur Studios - (Triceratops), 3ftr (Iguanodon), 8cb
(Triceratops); Robert L. Braun - modelmaker 1tl (Compsognathus), 2ca (Dilophosaurus), 2cb (Dimorphodon), 2fcr
(Lesothosaurus), 5cl (Stegosaurus), 7tc (Styracosaurus), 8bl (Dilophosaurus);
Graham High at Centaur Studios - modelmaker 4fbr (Triceratops), 5tr (Brachiosaurus), 7ftr (T-rex);
Jon Hughes / Bedrock Studios 3clb (Dryosaurus), 4tc (Therizinosaurus), 5cr (Giganotosaurus), 5tl
(Metriorhynchus), 7cr (Camarsaurus); Natural History Museum, London 1cl (horn), 1cra (skull), 1fbr (skull),
1fcr (bone), 1ftl (Psittacosaurus), 1tr (footprint), 2bl (skull), 2cr (skull), 2fcrb (foot), 3br (skull), 3cra (nest),
3fbl (plate), 3fcla (Archaeopteryx), 4c (skull), 4ca (tooth), 4cr (bone), 4fcr (skull), 4tl (teeth), 5bc (fossil),
5cra (bone), 5fbl (bone), 7cr (Heterodontosaurus), 8bc (horn), 8bl (tooth), 8cl (Pterodactylus); Jonathan
Hately - modelmaker 3cb (Baryonyx), 8ftr (Baryonyx); John Holmes - modelmaker 1fcla (Gallimimus), 1tc
(Hypsilophodon); John Holmes - modelmaker / Natural History Museum 2cla (nest); Jeremy Hunt at Centaur
Studios - modelmaker 6fcrb (Barosaurus); Hunterian Museum (University of Glasgow) 6tr (skeleton);
Naturmuseum Senckenburg, Frankfurt 3cl (skeleton); Luis Rey - modelmaker 4cr (Velociraptor); Royal Tyrrell
Museum of Palaeontology, Alberta, Canada 3ca (Dromaeosaurus), 3fclb (skeleton), 4ca (skeleton), 4cla (skull),
6fcra (skeleton), 6ftl (bone); Sedgwick Museum of Geology, Cambridge 8cla (Criorhynchus); Senckenberg
Nature Museum, Frankfurt 1bc (skeleton); Gary Staab - modelmaker 1fclb (Coelophysis). **Getty Images:** 3tc
(Nothronychus), 10ftr (Nothronychus), 15cl (Nothronychus), 16tr (Nothronychus); De Agostini Picture
Library / DEA Picture Library 7fbr (Wuerhosaurus), 12cra (Wuerhosaurus); Jonathan S. Blair / National
Geographic 2cr (skeleton), 9c (skeleton), 15clb (skeleton), 16cra (skeleton); O. Louis Mazzatenta / National
Geographic 1ca (skull), 2fbl (fossil), 2ftr (fossil), 9tl (fossil), 11tl (fossil), 12br (skull), 15fcl (skull), 16bc
(skull); Ira Block / National Geographic 6cl (fossil), 10clb (fossil), 13tl (fossil), 14clb (fossil), 15bl (fossil),
16cr (fossil); De Agostini Picture Library / DEA Picture Library / Barry Croucher 15cr (Scutellosaurus),
16bl (Scutellosaurus); DEA Picture Library 4fbl (Eustreptospondylus), 15ca (Eustreptospondylus), 16fclb
(Eustreptospondylus); National Geographic / Jeffrey L. Osborn 3tr (Masiakasaurus), 8ftl (Amargasaurus), 11fbr
(Masiakasaurus), 11ftr (Amargasaurus), 14bl (Amargasaurus), 14fclb (Masiakasaurus), 15cla (Masiakasaurus),
15cr (Dracorex), 15fcrb (Amargasaurus), 15ftl (Amargasaurus), 16bl (Dracorex), 16c (Amargasaurus), 16crb
(Masiakasaurus), 16tl (Amargasaurus); Spencer Platt 4clb (fossil), 12tc (fossil), 15br (fossil), 16cla (fossil);
Mario Tama 6br (skull), 10bl (skull), 13ftl (skull). **The Natural History Museum, London:** Anness
Publishing 6bl (Torvosaurus).

Jacket images: _Front:_ **DK Images:** Robert L. Braun - modelmaker bl, c; Jon Hughes / Bedrock Studios cra;
Natural History Museum, London ca, cla; Luis Rey - modelmaker bc. _Back:_ **DK Images:** Bedrock Studios clb;
Centaur Studios - modelmakers crb; John Holmes - modelmaker tc.

All other images © Dorling Kindersley **www.dkimages.com**

About this book

What's inside

This book is a fantastic introduction to the amazing world of dinosaurs. Not only will you have fun finding the right dinosaur stickers, but you will also learn lots of interesting facts, too.

How to use this book

Read the information pages and then search for the relevant stickers at the back of the book to fill in the gaps. Use the sticker outlines and labels to help you.

There are lots of extra stickers that you can use to decorate the scenes at the back of the book. It's up to you where you put them all. The most important thing is to have lots of sticker fun!

Contents

The age of dinosaurs

Earth formed about 4.6 billion years ago. Experts have divided the passage of time since into chunks called eras. The dinosaurs lived in the Mesozoic era, which is broken up into the Cretaceous, Jurassic, and Triassic periods. They lived for an astonishing 160 million years and died out 65 million years ago.

CRETACEOUS PERIOD
144–65 million years ago (mya)

Edmontonia

Velociraptor

Tyrannosaurus

JURASSIC PERIOD
208–144 (mya)

Brachiosaurus

Stegosaurus

Lesothosaurus

TRIASSIC PERIOD
250–208 (mya)

Plateosaurus

Herrerasaurus

FACT!
Dinosaurs have been found on all continents including Antarctica. Currently we know of about 500 kinds.

CLAW

TAIL

LEGS

SKIN

Anchisaurus

Eoraptor

Coelophysis

Giganotosaurus
(CRETACEOUS PERIOD)

Features

What makes a dinosaur? They all have scaly skin (some have feathers, too); long tails (used for balance and defense); legs that are held straight under the body; and claws.

Small carnivores

Not all meat-eating dinosaurs were the enormous, terrifying type that killed the big plant-eaters of the time. Some, like these, were very small and fed on smaller animals. But with their sharp teeth and claws they were still vicious.

Ornitholestes

This dinosaur gets its name, "bird robber," from its long grasping hands. It lived in the riverside forests of Jurassic North America.

Compsognathus

This little dinosaur was about the size of a chicken. Only two skeletons of *Compsognathus* have been found, one with a lizard's bones in its stomach. It lived along Europe's sea coast in the Jurassic period.

FACT!

When *Compsognathus* was found in 1861, experts originally thought it was too small to be a dinosaur.

Deinonychus

With sickle-shaped claws n each foot, this predator uld stand on one foot and slash at prey with the other.

Staurikosaurus

Speedy South American *Staurikosaurus* was one of the first carnivorous dinosaurs. Like all meat-eaters, it ran on its strong hind legs and had long jaws and sharp teeth.

Eoraptor

At a time when most of the world was desert, the dinosaurs evolved. *Eoraptor* ("dawn hunter") was one of the earliest. It lived in one of the few forests.

Coelophysis

Coelophysis was a long and slender fox-sized hunter, feeding on small animals. It lived in family groups in the desert in late Triassic or early Jurassic times.

DID YOU KNOW!

Small dinosaurs were more intelligent than large ones.

Shuvuuia

The strange thing about *Shuvuuia* was its forelimbs. They were short and stubby and ended in a single, clawed digit. It may have used this claw to dig into ants' nests.

Sinornithosaurus

We know this dinosaur from very well-preserved skeletons, which even show its feathers. Its sharp teeth and claws show it to have been a fierce hunter. It lived along the banks of the Chinese lakes.

Large carnivores

When we think of dinosaurs we usually imagine the big, ferocious, meat-eaters featured here. These famous beasts lived in different places at different times, but they all fed on the other dinosaurs existing alongside them.

FACT!
Small meat-eaters may have hunted in packs—big ones hunted alone.

Ceratosaurus

Ceratosaurus looked like a dragon, with a nose horn and jagged crest. It hunted in the riverside forests of the Jurassic period.

Dilophosaurus

This wolf-sized hunter (the biggest of its time) from the early Jurassic deserts carried two distinctive crests on its head—probably for showing off.

Learn more on page 10

Tyrannosaurus

With its huge slashing teeth, *Tyrannosaurus* was one of the last of the meat-eaters, prowling the woodlands of the Cretaceous period.

Torvosaurus

Torvosaurus was one of the biggest hunters in the Jurassic riverside forests—even bigger than its neighbor *Allosaurus*.

Spinosaurus

Spinosaurus lived in Africa in the early Cretaceous period. The tall sail on its back helped to keep it cool as it hunted in the tropical swamps.

DID YOU KNOW!

The original skeleton of *Spinosaurus* was lost when its museum was bombed during World War II.

Giganotosaurus

This cousin of *Allosaurus* may have been the longest meat-eater that ever lived, and could have swallowed you whole. It lived in South America in the late Cretaceous period. It was as heavy as an African elephant.

Learn more on page 11

Allosaurus

With its big clawed hands and its strong teeth, *Allosaurus* was the fiercest hunter in the Jurassic riverside forests. It was as heavy as a hippo.

Eustreptospondylus

In Jurassic times, when Europe consisted of a series of islands in a shallow sea, *Eustreptospondylus* prowled the shorelines looking for prey.

Tyrannosaurus

This is the most famous of the big meat-eating dinosaurs. With its enormous jaws and powerful teeth, it killed and ate the biggest plant-eaters of the time. It probably hid in the bushes and ambushed prey, bursting out and smashing into it with the full weight of its body.

Lived: 67–65 mya
Habitat: Woodland
Diet: Meat
Length: 39 ft (12 m)
Weight: 7 tons (6.5 metric tons)

NAME
How do you say it?
TIE-RAN-OH-SAW-RUS
What does it mean?
"Tyrant lizard"

TOOTH

SKULL

Skeleton

In 1915, the first *Tyrannosaurus* skeleton was mounted for public view in New York's American Museum of Natural History. Pieced together from the bones of three partial skeletons, it was standing upright like a kangaroo, instead of horizontally.

FOSSIL FINDS

North America

Asia

Allosaurus

Allosaurus was the biggest of the meat-eaters at the end of the Jurassic period. Unlike the later *Tyrannosaurus*, it had big strong arms with three huge claws on its fingers. It also had sharp claws on its feet.

Lived: 150–145 mya
Habitat: Riverside forest
Diet: Meat
Length: 39 ft (12 m)
Weight: 2–3 tons (1.8–2.7 metric tons)

FOOTPRINTS
Allosaurus and *Apatosaurus* footprints.

SKELETON

ADULT AND BABY TOOTH

FOSSIL FINDS

Europe and Africa

North America

NAME
How do you say it?
AL-OH-SAW-RUS
What does it mean?
"Different lizard"

Skull

The skull of *Allosaurus*, like that of most dinosaurs, was full of holes, and just made up of narrow strips of bone. This kept the weight of the head down and made it so flexible that it could gulp down huge chunks of meat. The teeth kept growing and dropping out when worn. They were replaced all the time by new ones.

FEEDING FRENZY
Allosaurus used its claws and teeth to rip flesh from other dinosaurs.

Other carnivores

There were many medium-sized meat-eating dinosaurs in the Triassic, Jurassic, and Cretaceous periods. Many other kinds of meat-eating animals lived there, too.

Fruitachampsa

Fruitachampsa, another crocodile, lived in the riverside forests of the Jurassic period. It was the size of a cat and hunted lizards and small mammals.

Rutiodon

Although *Rutiodon* looked like a crocodile, it belonged to a group called the phytosaurs that were only distantly related. It prowled the desert streams of Triassic times.

DID YOU KNOW?
A few of the medium-sized meat-eating dinosaurs were as intelligent as some of today's birds.

Postosuchus

In the Triassic deserts, when the dinosaurs were first appearing, the main hunters were land-dwelling crocodiles. Some, like *Postosuchus*, were as big as lions.

Tanycolagreus

A little smaller than its neighbor *Elaphrosaurus*, *Tanycolagreus* dodged between the feet of the great plant-eaters and hunted through the forest undergrowth.

Terrestrisuchus

The earliest crocodiles were not like modern water-dwellers. *Terrestrisuchus*, with its long legs, ran after small prey in the Triassic deserts.

Troodon

Turkey-sized *Troodon* is thought to have been one of the most intelligent dinosaurs of the Cretaceous woodlands. With its big eyes and sharp claws, it may have hunted, owl-like, in the evenings.

FACT!

Most meat-eating animals just before the dinosaurs were crocodile relatives.

Piatnitzkysaurus

This fast-moving meat-eater lived in South America in middle Jurassic times. It was not the biggest of the meat-eaters, but could tackle the young of the big plant-eating dinosaurs.

Elaphrosaurus

This agile, wolf-sized dinosaur was one of the medium-sized carnivores of the Jurassic riverside forests.

Food

Different dinosaurs ate different kinds of food. The earliest dinosaurs were all meat-eaters, feeding on smaller animals. Many later types became plant-eaters, feeding on ferns and trees. The later meat-eaters grew bigger and fed on the plant-eaters. It was a savage world!

MONKEY PUZZLE
An early tree eaten by vegetarian dinosaurs.

Dinosaur dung
We can learn a lot about the diets of dinosaurs and other ancient animals by looking at what is in their fossilized dung. Fossil dung is called coprolite.

IGUANODON
This plant-eater had a multipurpose hand. It walked on its three middle fingers. Its thumb was a spike for tearing down branches. The fifth finger could curl around to grasp food.

Fishing for food

Some dinosaurs ate fish. *Baryonyx* gets its name, "heavy claw," from this huge, hooklike claw on its thumb. It stood by the river and hooked fish out of the water, like grizzly bears do today.

Built to hunt

The shape of a meat-eating dinosaur—long jaws, sharp teeth, running legs, claws—made it ideal for hunting and killing the animals on which it fed.

GINGKO

This tree exists today, but fossils tell us that it dates back to dinosaur times. Many plant-eating dinosaurs fed on its fan-shaped leaves.

HIGH-RISE

Some long-necked dinosaurs, like *Brachiosaurus*, could lift their heads high into trees to reach the best leaves.

FACT!

Discoveries of fossilized dung show that mighty *Tyrannosaurus* ate horned dinosaurs.

Small vegetarians

With so many different types of plant living at the time of the dinosaurs, it is not surprising that there were all kinds of different dinosaurs that fed on them. Big dinosaurs usually ate food from high up in the trees, but small dinosaurs ate plants closer to the ground.

DID YOU KNOW? Small plant-eating dinosaurs had teeth like vegetable graters, for ripping up plants.

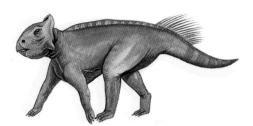

Cerasinops

Cerasinops was a badger-sized relative of the big horned dinosaurs and, like them, lived in the woodlands at the end of the Cretaceous period.

Psittacosaurus

This dinosaur gets its name, "parrot lizard," from the huge beak in the front of its jaws. It used this beak to break into tough plants.

Dryosaurus

Dryosaurus lived in the woodlands of what is now North America, Africa, and Europe. Its horny beak, at the front of the lower jaw, met with a toothless beak on the upper jaw. It was used for cropping.

Incisivosaurus

The big front teeth made *Incisivosaurus* look a little like a rabbit. Otherwise, it looked like a turkey. It would have used the teeth to feed on lake-shore vegetation.

Heterodontosaurus

Turkey-sized *Heterodontosaurus* had three different types of teeth—cutting teeth, chisel-like teeth and sharp tusks—all useful for feeding on sparse desert vegetation.

Stegoceras

Stegoceras had a thick bony skull and used it in head-butting battles with others of its herd, just as goats do today. Its teeth were great for shredding woodland undergrowth plants.

Pisanosaurus

We do not really know what *Pisanosaurus* looked like. Ideas about its appearance come from just a few scraps of bone. But we can tell it was one of the earliest plant-eating dinosaurs from the Triassic deserts.

FACT!
A plant-eater's body is larger than a meat-eater's because it needs a bigger and more complex digestive system.

Thecodontosaurus

Rabbit-sized *Thecodontosaurus* lived in the deserts of the Triassic period. It had a small head, long neck and tail, and saw-edged teeth. It was capable of walking on all four limbs.

More plant-eaters

There were lots of different kinds of medium-sized plant-eating dinosaur. Some of them belonged to the long-necked plant-eating group, and some of them belonged to the duckbill group (see p. 20).

(see p. 20).

DID YOU KNOW?
Dinosaurs existed for about a hundred times longer than humans have been on Earth.

Anchisaurus

Anchisaurus was one of the smaller long-necked plant-eaters. It lived in the deserts of Triassic times, and could rear up on its hind legs to feed from the trees in oases.

Massopondylus

This dinosaur was like *Anchisaurus*, but lived in Africa. It had a big claw on its forefoot (left) and used this to pull down leaves and branches from trees.

Maiasaura

Herds of this dinosaur nested together. We know this because experts have found their nests and babies in a site in Montana.

Learn more on page 19

Learn more on page 19

Ouranosaurus

Ouranosaurus was an amazing-looking animal! It had a big sail down its back and tail. The sail was used to keep it cool in the desert heat.

Maiasaura

The best-known dinosaur nests were made by the duckbill *Maiasaura*. These were found in the 1980s and show how dinosaurs brought up their youngsters.

Lived: 80–74 mya
Habitat: Coastal plains
Diet: Leaves
Length: 30 ft (9 m)
Weight: 5½ tons (5 metric tons)

FOSSIL FINDS

North America

FOSSIL NEST
This is a nest of baby duckbill dinosaurs found in the Gobi Desert, Mongolia.

SKELETON

INFANT

EGG NEST

Good parents

The nests of *Maiasaura* were built from mud, along the shores of lakes. When the youngsters hatched, the parents brought them food and looked after them. When they were big enough to walk, they migrated with the herd to the feeding grounds.

NAME
How do you say it?
MAY-A-SAW-RA
What does it mean?
"Good earth-mother lizard"

Large vegetarians

Toward the end of the dinosaur age, the main plant-eaters were large vegetarians called duckbills. These dinosaurs had mouths that were broad and flat at the front, but at the back there were lots of strong grinding teeth for dealing with tough vegetation.

DID YOU KNOW! Lambeosaurus had more than 1,000 teeth—all for chewing plants.

Learn more on page 21

Parasaurolophus
The crest on this dinosaur was used for making noises like a trombone, as it signaled to other dinosaurs in the woodlands where it lived.

Iguanodon
Iguanodon lived at an earlier time than the duck-billed dinosaurs on this page, and may have been their ancestor.

Lambeosaurus
Lambeosaurus was the same shape as *Parasaurolophus*. The different-shaped crest helped them recognize one another and kept the herds apart.

Corythosaurus
The crest of this duckbill was semicircular and looked a little like an ancient Greek helmet. It lived in the woodlands of the late Cretaceous period.

Iguanodon

Iguanodon was discovered in the 1820s. At first, only the fossil teeth—obviously belonging to a plant-eater—were found. The only plant-eating reptile known at that time was the iguana lizard, and so the fossil animal was named *Iguanodon*.

Lived: 135–125 mya
Habitat: Lake
Diet: Plants
Length: 30 ft (9 m)
Weight: 4½–5½ tons (4–5 metric tons)

SKULL

TEETH

NAME

How do you say it?
IG-WAH-NOH-DON
What does it mean?
"Iguana tooth"

Footprints

FOSSIL FINDS

Europe

Asia

North America

In the 1870s a whole herd of complete *Iguanodon* skeletons was found in Belgium, Europe. People could see for the first time what the whole animal was like. Since then, remains—including footprints—have been found all over the world.

Giant vegetarians

The long-necked plant-eating dinosaurs were the biggest land animals that ever lived. They were the most important plant-eaters in the first half of the age of dinosaurs. Later they became less common and were replaced by the duckbills.

Amargasaurus

This strange vegetarian from South America had a double row of long spines along its neck and a fin down its back. It probably used these to show off.

Alamosaurus

Alamosaurus was one of the last of the long-necked plant-eaters, roaming the woodlands of North America at the end of the Cretaceous period.

FACT!

Plant-eating dinosaurs had wide mouths for gathering leaves and big cheeks to hold large mouthfuls of food.

Camarasaurus

From North America, this dinosaur was the most common of the giant plant-eaters of the Jurassic riverside forests. Its skull was distinctively short and boxlike, and it had huge nostrils.

Argentinosaurus

This was the biggest of the giant vegetarians. Some of its vertebrae were as tall as a man, and the whole animal probably weighed about 110 tons (100 metric tons).

DID YOU KNOW!

Some plant-eaters swallowed stones to help them grind up their food.

Apatosaurus

Apatosaurus was the best-known of the giant vegetarians from the riverside forests of the Jurassic period. When it was first studied over 130 years ago it was given the name *Brontosaurus*.

Barosaurus

This had one of the longest necks of any dinosaur. It could sweep its tiny head around like the hose of a vacuum cleaner and collect food from a wide area.

Learn more on page 24

Diplodocus

Diplodocus used its incredibly long tail as a whip to keep enemies away. Along with *Barosaurus* and *Apatosaurus*, it fed on the low vegetation of the riverside forests.

Brachiosaurus

Brachiosaurus lived alongside *Apatosaurus*, but whereas *Apatosaurus* fed from low-growing vegetation, *Brachiosaurus*, with its tall shoulders and long neck, ate from the tops of the trees.

Diplodocus

Diplodocus is one of the longest of the known dinosaurs. For all its length it was quite lightweight. Its long neck enabled it to reach out for food over a wide area, and its long tail was used like a whip.

Lived: 155–145 mya
Habitat: Riverside forest
Diet: Leaves
Length: 87 ft (27 m)
Weight: 13 tons (12 metric tons)

NAME

How do you say it?
DIP-LOD-OH-KUS
What does it mean?
"Double beam"

FOSSIL FINDS

North America

Skeleton

We know a lot about *Diplodocus* from the many skeletons found. The head, as big as a horse's, has narrow jaws with comblike teeth—it just raked up its food and swallowed, without chewing. Its tail bones had skidlike structures beneath them, to protect the tail if it dragged on the ground. The backbones were full of air spaces, to keep the skeleton light.

TAIL SKID

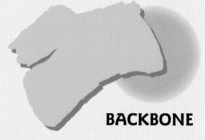

BACKBONE

Other vegetarians

It was not just the dinosaurs that ate the plants of the Triassic, Jurassic, and Cretaceous periods. All kinds of other animals lived in those times as well, and many competed with them for food.

Placerias

Placerias lived in the oases of the Triassic deserts. Its long tusks helped it to dig up roots, and its turtlelike beak could break off tough stems.

Desmatosuchus

In the Triassic deserts there lived animals that were related to crocodiles. *Desmatosuchus*, with its spiked shoulders and its piglike head, fed from low-growing plants.

Proganochelys

Turtles are a very old group of animals. They date back to *Proganochelys* that lived in the deserts of Triassic times. They had shells like modern turtles.

Macelognathus

This cat-sized animal was actually a kind of long-legged plant-eating crocodile. It had broad spade-shaped jaws and ate leaves from the ground plants of the Jurassic forests.

Habitats

The dinosaurs' world was very different from ours. There were no cities or fields or roads, in fact, nothing built by people. Mountains and seas were in different places, giving totally different landscapes. Even the plants were different—flowers only appeared at the very end of dinosaur times.

Sea

Riverside forest

Desert

Migration
Some dinosaurs, like other animals, migrated every year to find food or to reach their nesting sites as the seasons changed. These journeys would have been dangerous.

Lake

WHERE DINOSAURS ROAMED
A habitat is an area that animals and plants share, for example, sea, desert, lake, woodland plains, and riverside forest.

Woodland plains

HOME, SWEET HOME
Triceratops lived on
open plains.

FOSSILIZED FERN
Ferns took the place of
grasses during the
age of dinosaurs.

Camouflage
Some big plant-eaters were
probably colored green and
brown. They could hide from
meat-eaters among the plants
of the forests.

Landscapes
In early dinosaur times
the plants were all green and
brown, with no real flowers. In
the Cretaceous period, flowers
like magnolias and buttercups
appeared. The last dinosaurs
lived in a colorful world.

FACT!
Grass did not evolve
until very late in
dinosaur times. There
were no grassy
plains habitats.

Tree-dwellers

Some of the smallest dinosaurs could climb trees. We can tell this because fossils have been found with long toes and curved claws, like those of modern tree-dwelling birds.

Microraptor

This was the smallest dinosaur known. It lived by lakes and the feathers on its arms and legs allowed it to glide from tree to tree.

Archaeopteryx

Archaeopteryx was the first bird. It evolved from dinosaurs that climbed trees. It developed wings with flight feathers that helped it fly from tree to tree.

Epidendrosaurus

The long fingers (above) and toes of *Epidendrosaurus* show that it climbed trees, alongside its relatives *Microraptor* and *Scansoriopteryx*.

Scansoriopteryx

Scansoriopteryx was another tiny dinosaur. It may have had primitive wings that would have allowed it to glide. Like *Microraptor*, it lived around the lakes of early Cretaceous China.

Flying reptiles

Flying reptiles lived at the same time as the dinosaurs, but were only distantly related. Most of them were what we call pterosaurs. They had small furry bodies and broad leathery wings.

Eudimorphodon

Pterosaurs appeared at the same time as the first dinosaurs. *Eudimorphodon* was one of the earliest.

Anurognathus

This was one of the smallest of the pterosaurs. About the size of a sea gull, it hunted insects over Jurassic shorelines.

Icarosaurus

Before the pterosaurs evolved, lizardlike animals like *Icarosaurus* glided across the rocky crags of the Triassic deserts.

Dimorphodon

This pterosaur had a deep head and a long tail. Like the others, *Dimorphodon* had a furry body and leathery wings.

FACT!

Although pterosaurs could flap their wings to fly, they couldn't fly as efficiently as birds.

Flying reptiles

The pterosaurs varied as much as modern birds do—some were tiny and others were massive. The wings were formed of skin supported on a very long fourth finger that was as strong as the arm.

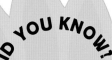

Quetzalcoatlus

The biggest pterosaur known is *Quetzalcoatlus*. It flew above the woodlands of late Cretaceous North America.

Criorhynchus

Criorhynchus was a large pterosaur, with a wingspan like an albatross. It soared over the ocean in Cretaceous times.

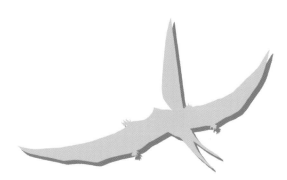

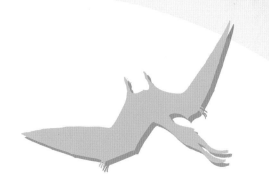

Nyctosaurus

This strange pterosaur lived in the air above the oceans at the end of the Cretaceous period. It had a crest on its head that looked like a third wing.

Pterodaustro

This flying reptile is called the pterosaur flamingo. Its jaws were armed with brushlike bristles and it filtered tiny animals from ponds, just like flamingos do.

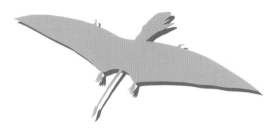

Sinopterus

About the size of a pigeon, *Sinopterus* fed on insects and plant material from the trees that overhung the lakes of early Cretaceous China.

Peteinosaurus

This was the earliest of the pterosaurs and flew above the deserts of Triassic times. Like other primitive types, such as *Rhamphorhynchus*, it had a long stiff tail.

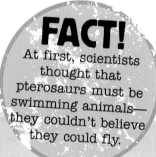

FACT!
At first, scientists thought that pterosaurs must be swimming animals— they couldn't believe they could fly.

Pterodactylus

Pterodactylus lived in the same time and place as *Rhamphorhynchus*, but it was less primitive. This and all the later pterosaurs had short tails.

Rhamphorhynchus

Rhamphorhynchus had long toothy jaws and a long stiff tail. A paddle on the end of the tail helped it to steer.

Sea reptiles

Dinosaurs did not live in the water, but when the dinosaurs were the rulers of the land there were all kinds of strange reptiles that lived in the sea. Some of these were as big and fierce as the dinosaurs themselves.

Ichthyosaurus

The name *Ichthyosaurus* means "fish-lizard" and describes it perfectly. Even though it was a reptile it had a fishlike body and tail, a fin on its back, and its limbs were swimming paddles.

Metriorhynchus

Some of the crocodiles of dinosaur times became sea-going animals. *Metriorhynchus* was so well adapted to a swimming way of life it had a fishlike tail fin and flippers for limbs.

FACT!
The fossils of sea-dwelling animals are more common than those of land-dwellers like dinosaurs.

Cryptoclidus

Related to the pliosaurs, the plesiosaurs were long-necked fish-eating reptiles with little heads and sharp teeth. *Cryptoclidus* was a typical plesiosaur.

Liopleurodon

Liopleurodon belonged to a group of huge swimming reptiles called the pliosaurs. They cruised the oceans hunting for prey. Their limbs evolved into winglike flippers, like the wings of penguins.

Freshwater reptiles

A whole range of swimming reptiles lived in the rivers and lakes of dinosaur times. These were mostly much smaller than their dinosaur relatives, but some were real giants.

Champsosaurus

Although *Champsosaurus* looked like a crocodile, it was only distantly related. It lived in the Jurassic and Cretaceous rivers and snapped up fish with its long jaws.

Deinosuchus

This was the biggest crocodile that ever lived. It existed at the end of the Cretaceous period and ate dinosaurs that came to the rivers to drink.

DID YOU KNOW!
All land animals evolved from water animals. Some, like those shown here, returned to the water.

Tanytrachelos

This long-necked reptile lived in the ponds and desert streams of the Triassic period, swimming with its strong tail and long hind legs, feeding on insects and other small animals.

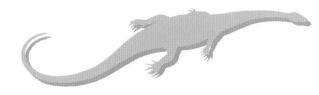

Hyphalosaurus

This reptile was like a lizard with a long neck. It used its webbed feet for swimming in the lakes of Cretaceous China.

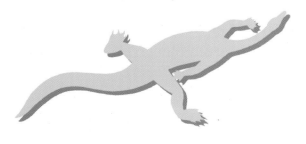

Eggs, nests, and young

All dinosaurs laid eggs, and some built nests like birds. The baby developed in the egg until it was ready to hatch. Dinosaur eggs had hard shells, but some reptile eggs—such as those of the flying pterosaurs—had leathery shells, similar to crocodile eggs.

Oviraptor egg

Oviraptor nests found in Mongolia show that the eggs were laid in a spiral. Each egg was about 6 in (16 cm) long.

OVIRAPTOR NEST
Like modern birds, *Oviraptor* spread its feathered body over its eggs to warm them.

Just hatched

Most dinosaurs, when first hatched, were small and helpless. The parents would look after them, bringing them food and defending them, until they were big enough to leave the nest.

Fossilized nest

It is hard to match dinosaurs to particular fossil eggs. These, from Montana, were thought to have been laid by a duck-billed dinosaur. Now experts believe they are from a meat-eater.

FACT!

The biggest dinosaur egg ever found—18 in (46 cm) long—was laid by a long-necked plant-eater.

TINY BABY

This newborn *Mussaurus* ("mouse lizard") is one of the smallest dinosaur specimens ever found. It emerged from a 1 in- (2.5 cm-) long egg, and the adult would have been 10 ft (3 m) long.

Feathered

A few perfectly fossilized skeletons show that at least some small dinosaurs were covered in feathers. The feathers were not for flying, but for warmth.

Oviraptor

We know this turkey-sized dinosaur from many skeletons, one of which has been found sitting on eggs in a nest. This is one of its eggs.

Therizinosaurus

This strange animal was related to the meat-eaters, but was a plant-eater. It used its big claws to pull branches down from trees.

DID YOU KNOW!
The claws of Therizinosaurus were about 36 in (90 cm) long—about the size of a man's arm.

Epidexipteryx

This small chicken-sized meat-eater, from the shores of Chinese lakes, had an unusual arrangement of plumes on its tail.

Dromaeosaurus

The name means "running lizard," and this active hunter was related to *Velociraptor*, hunting small animals in the woodlands of North America.

Caudipteryx

Caudipteryx had fanlike bunches of feathers on its arms and tail. It used these to signal to other animals on the lake banks.

Nothronychus

This was a smaller relative of *Therizinosaurus* and lived in the woodlands of late Cretaceous North America. It also had long claws and ate leaves.

FACT!

Dinosaur feathers were more like bunches of fuzzy hair than bird feathers.

Velociraptor

Velociraptor was about the size of a wolf, and like a wolf it hunted in packs. Several of them would hunt together to bring down a big plant-eater.

Sinosauropteryx

We can actually see the feathers on the fossil of *Sinosauropteryx*, since it was preserved in mud at the bottom of a lake in the early Cretaceous period.

Fur and feathers

Mammals and birds were around during the time of the dinosaurs. The birds brightened up the landscape with their colorful plumage, but the mammals were probably mostly hidden, camouflaged by their mousy-colored fur.

Confuciusornis

If you saw *Confuciusornis* flying over the lakes of Cretaceous China you would think it was a modern bird, with long tail-feathers. But it had dinosaurlike claws on its wings.

Oligokyphus

The mammals evolved from a group of animals known as "mammal-like reptiles." Some of these, like *Oligokyphus*, looked just like mammals, but still had reptile features in their skeleton.

DID YOU KNOW!
Three-quarters of all types of bird and mammal became extinct along with the dinosaurs.

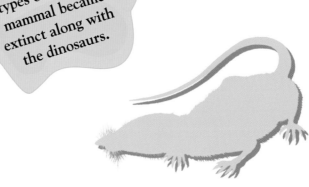

Fruitafossor

Burrowing into the riverbanks of the Jurassic forests, *Fruitafossor* kept out of the way of the big dinosaurs and hunted worms and burrowing insects.

Cimolestes

Rat-sized *Cimolestes* fed on insects in the woodland trees at the end of the Cretaceous period. It survived into the beginning of the age of mammals, once the dinosaurs became extinct.

FACT!
The first mammals appeared at the same time as the first dinosaurs.

Yanornis

Most birds that lived around the early Cretaceous lakes showed a mixture of bird features and dinosaur features. The size of a pigeon, *Yanornis* was probably the ancestor of modern birds, but it had teeth in its jaws.

Hesperornis

The bones of this bird show that it was a flightless sea-dweller, swimming after fish like a modern penguin. It lived among the great sea reptiles of the end of the Cretaceous period.

Repenomamus

Most mammals during dinosaur times were tiny—about mouse-sized. *Repenomamus* was much bigger— about the size of a badger—and it ate baby dinosaurs.

Schowalteria

In the woodlands of the very end of the age of dinosaurs lived mammals like *Schowalteria*, ready to take over as soon as the dinosaurs disappeared.

Fish-eaters

During dinosaur times, rivers and lakes were full of fish. Some dinosaurs evolved to hunt these. Experts can identify fish-eating animals by their teeth and claws, which are suited for catching slippery prey. Fossilized fish bones have also been found in their stomachs.

DID YOU KNOW!
Most modern sea birds eat fish. It is not surprising, therefore, that some of their ancestors, the dinosaurs, did too.

Masiakasaurus

The fossils of this dinosaur were found in Madagascar, Africa. The teeth at the front of the mouth were ideal for snapping up fish from rivers.

Suchomimus

Suchomimus was like a large version of *Baryonyx*, but with a low sail right down its back. It lived in Africa at the same time as *Baryonyx* lived in Europe.

Learn more on page 41

Baryonyx

Baryonyx lived in the marshes of the early Cretaceous period. It had an unusual crocodile-shaped skull and its huge, curved thumb claw—about 12 in (30 cm) long—was ideal for catching fish.

Parasuchus

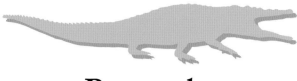

Parasuchus was neither a dinosaur nor a crocodile—it belonged to a group called the phytosaurs. Like a crocodile, it lived in water and hunted fish in Triassic times.

Baryonyx

Discovered in the 1970s, *Baryonyx* was the first fish-eating dinosaur known. Although it was well adapted to catching and eating fish, it did eat other things as well. Parts of *Iguanodon* bones were found in its stomach along with fish scales.

Lived: 125 mya
Habitat: Riverbanks
Diet: Fish
Length: 33 ft (10 m)
Weight: 2 tons (2 metric tons)

CLAW

FOOT

SKULL

FOSSIL FINDS

Europe

NAME
How do you say it?
BAR-EE-ON-ICKS
What does it mean?
"Heavy claw"

Skeleton

Everything about the skeleton of *Baryonyx* tells us that it was a fishing animal. The jaws were long and narrow, like those of a fish-eating crocodile. The many teeth were small and pointed—ideal for catching and holding slippery prey—and the huge hooklike claw on its thumb would have been used for snatching fish out of the water.

Fast runners

Small meat-eating dinosaurs were fast runners. They had to be to catch their food. And, of course, most of the small plant-eating dinosaurs had to be fast runners, too—so that they could escape them.

Ornithomimus

Ornithomimus was not only the size of an ostrich, but it also looked like one, too. With its long legs, it dodged between woodland trees and sprinted across plains.

Lesothosaurus

This was one of the earliest two-footed plant-eaters. It was no bigger than a large lizard and lived in the African deserts.

DID YOU KNOW?
Gallimimus, Ornithomimus, and *Struthiomimus* could all run about as fast as a racehorse.

Herrerasaurus

Fox-sized *Herrerasaurus* was one of the earliest meat-eaters from the deserts of South America. It chased small animals like lizards.

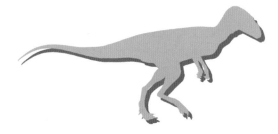

Hypsilophodon

Called the "gazelle of the dinosaur world," *Hypsilophodon* had strong running legs to help it escape the big meat-eaters that lived in Europe at the beginning of the Cretaceous period.

FACT!
The smallest dinosaur footprints ever discovered came from a dinosaur as small as a sparrow.

Bambiraptor

A cute name for an animal that was anything but cute! *Bambiraptor* was a vicious little hawk-sized hunter that chased small prey through the Cretaceous woodlands.

Struthiomimus

Like its neighbor *Ornithomimus*, *Struthiomimus* was like an ostrich. They both lived in North America in late Cretaceous times.

Chindesaurus

Most of the meat-eating dinosaurs of the Triassic and early Jurassic deserts were small, fast-running animals. Like *Chindesaurus*, they could chase their prey over rocks and dry sand.

Gallimimus

Gallimimus was a long-legged runner, related to *Ornithomimus* and *Struthiomimus*. It was a little larger than the other two and lived in Asia rather than North America.

Hunting and defense

I n the animal world, plant-eaters eat the plants and meat-eaters eat the plant-eaters. It was the same in dinosaur times. Some of the meat-eating dinosaurs were such ferocious hunters that the plant-eaters evolved all kinds of body weaponry in order to protect themselves.

LOCKED IN BATTLE

These skeletons of *Velociraptor* and *Protoceratops* are fossilized together. They fought each other to the death.

TALL TAILS

Some dinosaur tails were used as weapons.

Stegosaurus had long spikes on the end of its tail for jabbing at prey.

Armored

Gastonia was built like a tank and covered in bony studs for armor. Wicked spikes jutted out from its sides and its shoulders to keep fierce meat-eaters away.

Euoplocephalus had a club of fused bone at the end of its tail to swing at predators.

Diplodocus used its long tail as a whip.

Deinonychus

Deinonychus or "terrible claw" got its name from the killer claw on the second toe of each foot. They were used to slash at prey.

Warning signals

If in danger, *Parasaurolophus* could use its long crest—made from its nose bones—as a trumpet to make noises to warn the herd.

FACT!

Giganotosaurus may have slammed into its victims to knock them out with its body weight, before eating them.

ALLOSAURUS

This terrifying predator had special joints in its jaw that enabled it to open its mouth extra wide and gulp down the flesh of its victims.

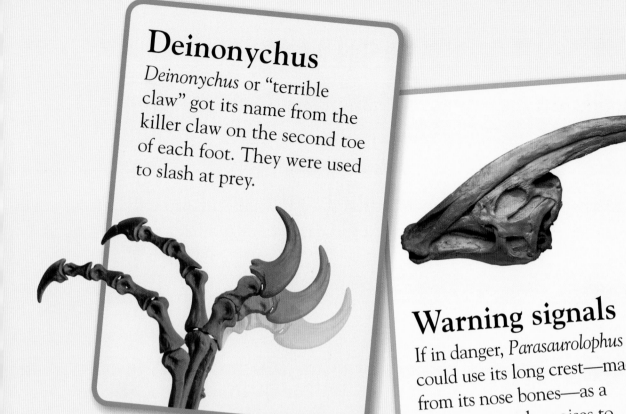

Plated dinosaurs

Some plant-eating dinosaurs had plates on their backs instead of armor. These plates may have been used as weapons or they may have been for showing off. Most of them lived in the late Jurassic and early Cretaceous periods.

DID YOU KNOW! The plates on dinosaurs were not attached to their skeletons—just embedded in the skin.

Dacenturus

Dacenturus had small plates over the back and neck, but long spikelike plates over the hips and tail. It lived in Europe in Jurassic times.

Learn more on page 47

Stegosaurus

Stegosaurus was the biggest and best-known of the plated dinosaurs. It lived in the riverside forests of late Jurassic North America.

Gigantspinosaurus

As its name suggests, this dinosaur had gigantic spines. They swept sideways from the shoulders like great wings and were used as defense against the meat-eaters of the Chinese plains.

Wuerhosaurus

One of the last of the plated dinosaurs was *Wuerhosaurus*, with its long, low plates. It was almost as big as *Stegosaurus* and lived in China.

Stegosaurus

Stegosaurus had a double row of plates down its back, some of them rounded and some pointed. At the end of its tail it carried two pairs of spikes for defense. Its head was tiny and it had the smallest brain of any dinosaur.

Lived: 155–144 mya
Habitat: Riverside forest
Diet: Plants
Length: 20 ft (6 m)
Weight: 2 tons (2 metric tons)

NAME

How do you say it?
STEG-OH-SAW-RUS
What does it mean?
"Roof lizard"

FOSSIL FINDS

Europe

North America

Skeleton

Dozens of *Stegosaurus* skeletons exist, and from these we can tell that the plates were made of bony slabs covered in skin. The tail spikes were sharp weapons covered in horn, which *Stegosaurus* used to swing at enemies. The teeth had coarse serrations on them for shredding plants.

TOOTH

PLATE FOSSIL

TAIL SPIKE

Horned dinosaurs

The big-horned dinosaurs had different numbers of horns arranged in different patterns on their heads. This helped them recognize each other and keep to their own herd—like the various types of antelope in Africa today.

Centrosaurus

Like *Styracosaurus*, also from the Cretaceous woodlands, *Centrosaurus* had a single big horn on the nose. But it did not have the long spikes around the frill.

Styracosaurus

You would always be able to recognize a *Styracosaurus*, because of the long spikes that jutted out from the back of its neck frill. It had a single horn on its nose.

FACT!

The dinosaur horns mentioned here were like those of cows—bony cores covered in horn.

Leptoceratops

Leptoceratops, the size of a small sheep, was one of the small primitive horned dinosaurs. It lived in the Cretaceous woodlands along with its big relatives.

Chasmosaurus

This horned dinosaur had the biggest neck frill of them all. It would have been brightly colored like a flag, and used for showing off to other dinosaurs in the Cretaceous woodlands.

DID YOU KNOW?

The earliest horned dinosaurs lived in Asia. The later ones only lived in North America.

Chaoyangsaurus

This primitive horned dinosaur was the size of a small goat. It walked on two legs and had a bunch of porcupinelike quills on the tail.

Albertaceratops

Scientists keep finding new species of horned dinosaur. *Albertaceratops* is one of the new ones—only named in 2007.

Hongshanosaurus

This, along with *Chaoyangsaurus*, was one of the earliest horned dinosaurs. They both lived by the lakes of early Cretaceous China.

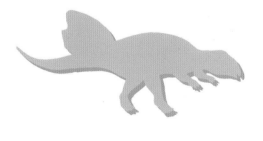

Learn more on page 50

Protoceratops

Like a camel, *Protoceratops* lived in herds in the desert. It used its parrotlike beak to eat the tough vegetation that it found there.

Protoceratops

The earliest horned dinosaurs like *Protoceratops* were small rabbit- or sheep-sized animals. They did not actually have any horns, but their heads were heavy and had the neck shields and big beaks of their bigger relatives.

Lived: 85–80 mya
Habitat: Desert
Diet: Plants
Length: 6 ft (1.8 m)
Weight: 400 lb (180 kg)

FOSSIL FINDS

Asia

NAME
How do you say it?
PRO-TOE-KER-A-TOPS
What does it mean?
"Before the horned faces"

ADULT SKULL

INFANT SKULL

Complete skeleton

Scientists have found whole herds of *Protoceratops* skeletons in the Gobi Desert, Mongolia. Many of them were complete and had been preserved when they were buried in sandstorms. This area of central Asia was desert even in Cretaceous times.

Triceratops

At the end of the Cretaceous period the horned dinosaurs became really big, and *Triceratops* was the biggest. It needed its neck shield and its three horns to protect itself from the big meat-eaters like *Tyrannosaurus*.

Lived: 70–65 mya
Habitat: Woodland
Diet: Plants
Length: 30 ft (9 m)
Weight: 5–11 tons (4.5–10 metric tons)

NAME
How do you say it?
TRY-SER-A-TOPS
What does it mean?
"Three-horned face"

Horns and shields

Triceratops, just like the other horned dinosaurs, had horns pointing forward. When danger came, *Triceratops* always turned to face it. That way it could protect its body with its neck shield.

FOSSIL FINDS

North America

HORN

SKULL

Armored

With so many big meat-eaters—like *Tyrannosaurus*—existing at the end of the dinosaur age, it is not surprising that many plant-eaters evolved armor and horns to protect themselves.

Ankylosaurus

Ankylosaurus was armored like a tank. Its main weapon was a club on the end of its tail, made from heavy bone. The vertebrae of the tail were fused together to form a stiff shaft.

Stygimoloch

In addition to a dome on its head for battering enemies, *Stygimoloch* had spikes all over its head. Like these other armored dinosaurs, it lived in the late Cretaceous woodlands.

FACT!

The weak spot on armored dinosaurs was their underbelly.

Triceratops

This is the most famous and the biggest of the horned dinosaurs. It had three horns: two long ones above the eyes and a smaller one on the nose.

Learn more on page 51

Euoplocephalus

Euoplocephalus had a club on its stiff straight tail, like its relative *Ankylosaurus*. Also its back was covered in horn-covered armor.

Pentaceratops

Some dinosaurs had horns rather than armor. The horns were mounted on the head and there was an armored frill protecting the neck. *Pentaceratops* had a huge frill that made its head look enormous.

Sauropelta

Sauropelta came earlier than the other armored dinosaurs on these two pages. Its main weapons were the rows of spikes on each side of the neck. Its back and long tail were also covered in armor.

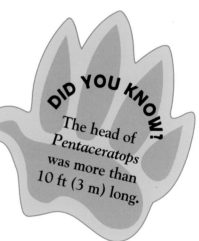

DID YOU KNOW?

The head of *Pentaceratops* was more than 10 ft (3 m) long.

Edmontonia

Edmontonia had most of its weapons on its shoulders. Huge spikes stuck out sideways and forward, so that it could charge at its enemies. There were also spikes along its sides and tail.

Gastonia

Gastonia's tail had a series of bladelike plates jutting sideways from it. As the tail curled, the plates slid over one another like scissor blades, cutting and injuring anything caught in between.

Fossils and finds

Dinosaurs have been extinct for tens of millions of years. We know what they were like from the remains that have been found preserved in rocks. Mostly, their fossils are of isolated scraps of bone, but sometimes whole skeletons are preserved.

Ghost Ranch

In a quarry in New Mexico, many small meat-eating *Coelophysis* were found fossilized together. They all died of thirst around a drying water hole during a drought.

LARGER THAN LIFE

This enormous *Tyrannosaurus* fossil was found in north-central South Dakota. It is about 65 million years old.

AMMONITE FOSSIL

Most fossils are of sea animals, like this ammonite. They are buried in seafloor mud and turned to rock.

Dinosaur National Monument

Sometimes dinosaurs were washed down rivers and fossilized where the currents tumbled them together. This site in Utah has 1,500 dinosaur fossils in a layer of river sandstone.

RARE HEAD

Dinosaur skulls do not often fossilize—they are too delicate. This *Gallimimus* skull is unusually complete.

HETERODONTOSAURUS

Heterodontosaurus skeleton fossilized in clay.

FACT!

"Fossil" comes from the Latin word *fossilis*. It means "dug up."

Lake

Checklist

Use the stickers in the book to fill up the scene. Here are some animals that you might find here. Which is your favorite?

- [ ] *Incisivosaurus*
- [ ] *Sinopterus*
- [ ] *Microraptor*
- [ ] *Epidendrosaurus*
- [ ] *Hyphalosaurus*
- [ ] *Sinosauropteryx*
- [ ] *Caudipteryx*
- [ ] *Confuciusornis*
- [ ] *Sinornithosaurus*
- [ ] *Repenomamus*

Woodland plains

Checklist

Use the stickers in the book to fill up the scene. Here are some animals that you might find here. Which is your favorite?

- [ ] *Tyrannosaurus*
- [ ] *Triceratops*
- [ ] *Troodon*
- [ ] *Ornithomimus*
- [ ] *Stygimoloch*
- [ ] *Parasaurolophus*
- [ ] *Quetzalcoatlus*
- [ ] *Nothronychus*
- [ ] *Schowalteria*
- [ ] *Ankylosaurus*

Riverside forest

Checklist

Use the stickers in the book to fill up the scene. Here are some animals that you might find here. Which is your favorite?

- [ ] *Fruitachampsa*
- [ ] *Allosaurus*
- [ ] *Elaphrosaurus*
- [ ] *Tanycolagreus*
- [ ] *Brachiosaurus*
- [ ] *Ornitholestes*
- [ ] *Diplodocus*
- [ ] *Apatosaurus*
- [ ] *Champsosaurus*
- [ ] *Stegosaurus*

Desert

Checklist

Use the stickers in the book to fill up the scene. Here are some animals that you might find here. Which is your favorite?

- [ ] *Coelophysis*
- [ ] *Dilophosaurus*
- [ ] *Rutiodon*
- [ ] *Anchisaurus*
- [ ] *Placerias*
- [ ] *Desmatosuchus*
- [ ] *Peteinosaurus*
- [ ] *Icarosaurus*
- [ ] *Oligokyphus*
- [ ] *Scutellosaurus*

Sea

Checklist

Use the stickers in the book to fill up the scene. Here are some animals that you might find here. Which is your favorite?

- [ ] *Ichthyosaurus*
- [ ] *Cryptoclidus*
- [ ] *Liopleurodon*
- [ ] *Metriorhynchus*
- [ ] *Compsognathus*
- [ ] *Anurognathus*
- [ ] *Pterodactylus*
- [ ] *Rhamphorhynchus*
- [ ] *Archaeopteryx*
- [ ] *Dacenturus*

Herrerasaurus

Gallimimus

Psittacosaurus

Edmontonia

Coelophysis

Triceratops horn

Icarosaurus

Compsognathus

Stegosaurus skeleton

Champsosaurus

Triceratops

Incisivosaurus skull

Caudipteryx

Hypsilophodon

Hongshanosaurus

Gastonia

Protoceratops adult skull

Iguanodon footprint

Diplodocus skull

Hesperornis centrum

Albertaceratops

Thecodontosaurus

Ceratosaurus

Shuvuuia

Sinosauropteryx fossil

Maiasaura nest

Corythosaurus

Sauropelta

Proganochelys skull

Eoraptor

Cerasinops

Dimorphodon

Argentinosaurus

Iguanodon skull

Dilophosaurus

Anurognathus

Desmatosuchus

Placerias skeleton

Massospondylus claw

Iguanodon foot

Lesothosaurus

Confuciusornis fossil

Stegosaurus
plate fossil

Ornithomimus
skeleton

Baryonyx foot

Archaeopteryx

Baby duckbill fossilized nest

Parasuchus

Barosaurus

Dryosaurus

Tyrannosaurus
skeleton

Baryonyx thumb
claw

Centrosaurus

Repenomamus

Suchomimus

Dromaeosaurus
skeleton

Nothronychus

Hyphalosaurus

Yanornis

Masiakasaurus

Protoceratops
infant skull

Oviraptor egg

Maiasaura nest

Apatosaurus

Gigantspinosaurus

Iguanodon

ustreptospondylus

Diplodocus

Microraptor fossil

Lambeosaurus head

Iguanodon teeth

Spinosaurus

Alamosaurus

Triceratops skeleton

Ornitholestes skeleton

Protoceratops

Tyrannosaurus skull

Tyrannosaurus tooth

Macellognathus

Scansoriopteryx

Therizinosaurus

Chaoyangsaurus

Stegosaurus tail spike

Oligokyphus

Velociraptor

Epidexipteryx

Triceratops

Triceratops skull

Protoceratops skeleton

Diplodocus
backbone

Ichthyosaurus

Allosaurus
skeleton

Baryonyx skull

Eudimorphodon

Fruitafossor

Stegosaurus

Metriorhynchus

Cimolestes

Struthiomimus

Terrestrisuchus

Schowalteria

Baryonyx

Chindesaurus

Deinosuchus

Diplodocus
tail skid

Parasaurolophus
skeleton

Brachiosaurus

Chasmosaurus
skeleton

Giganotosaurus

Allosaurus

Ouranosaurus

Rutiodon

Dacenturus

Ankylosaurus
tail club

Torvosaurus

Liopleurodon

Pterodaustro

Epidendrosaurus fingers

Baryonyx

Pisanosaurus

Sinopterus

Anchisaurus

Pentaceratops

Leptoceratops

Deinonychus

Cryptoclidus
skeleton

Stygimoloch
skull

Protoceratops

Diplodocus

Maiasaura skeleton

Allosaurus and
Apatosaurus footprints

Piatnitzkysaurus

Peteinosaurus

Fruitachampsa

Euoplocephalus

Rhamphorhynchus

Tanycolagreus

Bambiraptor

Stegoceras

Tyrannosaurus

Staurikosaurus

Allosaurus teeth

Styracosaurus

Elaphrosaurus

Heterodontosaurus

Postosuchus

Troodon

Camarasaurus

Wuerhosaurus

Allosaurus

Tyrannosaurus

Quetzalcoatlus

Sinornithosaurus

Amargasaurus

Maiasaura
infant

Nyctosaurus

Criorhynchus

Stegosaurus
tooth

Pterodactylus

Tanytrachelos